WE SHALL LIVE IN PEACE

WE SHALL LIVE IN PEACE:

The Teachings of Martin Luther King Jr.

Edited and with commentary by Deloris Harrison

Illustrated by Ernest Crichlow

Hawthorn Books, Inc.   Publishers   New York

WE SHALL LIVE IN PEACE

First Edition: 1968
Second Printing: 1969

Design: Gene Gordon

Thanks are extended to Joan Daves for permission to reprint "I Have a Dream," copyright © 1963 by Martin Luther King Jr. and to Harper & Row, Publishers, for permission to reprint portions of "Letter from Birmingham Jail," copyright © 1963 by Martin Luther King Jr. and "Stride Toward Freedom," copyright © 1958 by Martin Luther King Jr.

DEDICATION

To Medgar Evers, Viola Liuzzo, James Chaney, Michael Schwerner, Andrew Goodman and to the memory of all the others who died in the nonviolent struggle for full equality and brotherhood.

CONTENTS

INTRODUCTION

The words of Reverend Doctor Martin Luther King Jr. rang out across America and spanned the seas that separate us from Asia and Africa, from Europe and South America. They challenged the voices of hatred and prejudice with a new belief in love and human dignity. Through these teachings we learn of the black people's struggle to gain justice and equality in America. In these speeches Dr. King tells of his goals and ideals.

From the pulpit, from a jail cell, and from the heart of the Southland which he loved, Dr. King spoke to all men of goodwill.

TIME TABLE

1929   King, Michael (later changed to Martin Luther King Jr.) born January 15 in Atlanta, Georgia; second child and first son of Martin Luther King Sr. and Alberta Williams.

1944   Entered Morehouse College.

1948   Graduated from Morehouse College.

1948-51   Entered Crozer Theological Seminary, Chester, Pa. Studied and read the Greek philosophers, Thoreau, and Gandhi. Became president of the senior class.

1951-53   Received fellowship from Boston University to study for doctorate in Systematic Theology. Also took courses in philosophy at Harvard. Began courtship of Coretta Scott.

1953   June 18, married Coretta Scott on her father's lawn in Marion, Alabama.

1954   September 1, began service as pastor of Dexter Avenue Baptist Church in Montgomery, Alabama.

1955-56   Montgomery bus boycott. First use of nonviolent protest by Negroes.

1958   Stabbed by mentally ill Negro woman while autographing his book in a Harlem department store.

1959   Made pilgrimage to India to visit tomb of Mahatma Gandhi and to further study his principles of nonviolence.

1960	Created the Southern Christian Leadership Conference and was president. Jailed for not having a driver's license. John F. Kennedy, who was campaigning for the presidency, telephoned Mrs. King, promising to intercede.
1961	Jailed again in protest move against segregation in Albany, Georgia. Hundreds of others go to jail also.
1963	April. Dr. King arrested in Birmingham, Alabama—the target for mass demonstrations against segregation. Use of police dogs, fire hoses, and bombings bring world attention to the civil rights movement.
1963	Dr. King speaks at the march on Washington, organized to demonstrate the solidarity of the civil rights movement and to bring Negro grievances to the seat of government.
1964	December 10, received Nobel Prize for Peace.
1965	Voters registration drive and march from Selma to Montgomery, Alabama; faced with court injunction, police resistance, shootings, and beatings. Three thousand arrested including Dr. King. This was his seventeenth arrest.
1965-67	Carried campaign for equal rights for Negroes to the North. Actively opposed the war in Vietnam.
1967-68	Planned the Poor People's March on Washington to seek legislation to improve conditions.
1968	April 4. Assassinated in Memphis, Tennessee. Dr. King is survived by his widow, Mrs. Coretta King, and his four children: Yolanda, age 13; Martin III, age 11; Dexter, age 7; Bernice, age 5.

WE SHALL LIVE IN PEACE

THE BEGINNING: MONTGOMERY BUS BOYCOTT

In Montgomery, Alabama, in 1955, black people had very few rights and privileges. Places of public accommodation such as restaurants, public rest rooms, and buses were segregated. Segregated buses were one of the greatest indignities the Negroes had to suffer. A city ordinance required Negroes to ride in the back of buses and to give up their seats to whites if the bus was full. Very often the bus drivers were rude and unkind to Negroes. If they complained, they were arrested and fined.

One evening in December 1955, Mrs. Rosa Parks, a Negro seamstress, was coming home from a long day's work in a department store. She took a seat in the colored section of the bus, but at the next stop more white people got on and the bus driver told her to get up and give her seat to a white passenger. Mrs. Parks quietly refused. She was taken off the bus and arrested. This outraged the Negroes and sparked the community into action.

For the first time, they decided to unite to oppose injustice. They said that they would boycott the buses until changes were made. As their leader, they chose the young pastor of the Dexter Avenue Baptist Church, Reverend Martin Luther King, Jr.

December 5, 1955, was the day the boycott began. All day long, Dr. and Mrs. King, with the infant Yolanda in her arms, watched bus after bus go by empty. The hastily organized boycott was succeeding. That night at the Holt Street Baptist Church, Martin Luther King Jr. spoke out, saying:

There comes a time when people get tired. We are here this evening to say to those who have mistreated us so long that we are tired—tired of being segregated and humiliated; tired of being kicked about by the brutal feet of oppression. . . .

For many years, we have shown amazing patience. We have sometimes given our white brothers the feeling that we liked the way we were being treated. But we come here tonight to be saved from that patience that makes us patient with anything less than freedom and justice. One of the great glories of democracy is the right to protest for right. . . .

There will be no threats and intimidation. We will be guided by the highest principles of law and order. Our method will be that of persuasion, not coercion. . . . Our actions must be guided by the deepest principles of our Christian faith. Love must be our regulating ideal. . . . If we fail to do this our protest will end up as a meaningless drama on the stage of history, and its memory will be shrouded with the ugly garments of shame. In spite of the mistreatment that has confronted us, we must not become bitter, and end up by hating our white brothers. . . .

If you will protest courageously, and yet with dignity and Christian love, then when the history books are written in future generations, the historians will have to pause and say, "There lived a great people—a black people—who injected new meaning and dignity into the veins of civilization." This is our challenge and our overwhelming responsibility.

VIOLENCE:
THE DESTROYER

*F*rom the beginning of the nonviolent crusade for Negro rights, there had been terrible acts of violence by those who opposed it. Acts of violence were carried out not only by individual members of the white community but by the police as well.

Trying to break up demonstrations and discourage sit-ins and marches by supporters of integration, the police of cities such as Montgomery and Birmingham used fire hoses and police dogs. Neither women nor children were spared.

Many (both white and black) who believed in the rights of the Negro gave their lives for this cause. In Birmingham, Alabama, on September 16, 1963, four Negro children were killed when a bomb exploded in a church. This was the twenty-first bombing in this city. In March 1965, after the Selma to Montgomery march was over, a white housewife, Mrs. Viola Liuzzo, was shot. And in Philadelphia, Mississippi, in 1964, three young men—two whites, one Negro—were brutally slain.

Martin Luther King Jr. was also threatened and his home was bombed. His name, which became synonymous with the civil rights movement, was hated by those who hated the movement.

Dr. King was deeply disturbed by all these tragedies. He spoke out in order to give comfort and understanding to all men of goodwill:

After the bombing of his home: Montgomery, 1956

If you have weapons, take them home; if you do not have them, please do not seek to get them. We cannot solve this problem through retaliatory violence. We must meet violence with nonviolence. Remember the words of Jesus: "He who lives by the sword will perish by the sword." We must love our white brothers, no matter what they do to us. We must make them know that we love them. . . . We must meet hate with love. Remember if I am stopped, this movement will not stop, because God is with the movement. Go home with this glowing faith and this radiant assurance.

Telegram to the President on the death of the four little girls: September 16, 1963

[I will] plead with my people to remain nonviolent in the face of this terrible provocation. I am convinced that unless some immediate steps are taken by the Federal Government to restore a sense of confidence in the protection of life, limb and property, my pleas will fall on deaf ears and we shall see in Birmingham and Alabama the worst racial holocaust the nation has ever seen. . . .

The lives of women and children are far more precious than the offense created by the elimination of outmoded customs and traditions. . . .

After today's tragedy, investigation alone will not suffice. The Nation and Birmingham need your commitment to use everything within your power to enforce the desegregation orders of the court. . . .

To the Governor of the State of Alabama: September 16, 1963

The blood of four little children and others critically injured is on your hands. . . . Your irresponsible and misguided actions have created the atmosphere that has induced continued violence and murder.

At the funeral of the little girls: September 1963

Good still has a way of growing out of evil. The blood of these girls must serve as a revitalizing force to bring light to this dark city. . . .

Montgomery, Alabama, March 25, 1965

We are on the move now. The burning of churches will not deter us. We are on the move now. The bombing of our homes will not dissuade us. We are on the move now. The beating and killing of our clergymen and young people will not divert us. We are on the move now. The arrest and release of known murderers will not discourage us. We are on the move now. Like an idea whose time has come not even the marching of mighty armies can halt us. We are moving to the land of freedom. . . .

NONVIOLENCE:
A SWORD THAT HEALS

While still in Crozer Theological Seminary, Dr. King began to read about nonviolence in the writings of Mahatma Gandhi. Gandhi had helped his people in India gain their freedom by marches, sit-ins, fasts, and other peaceful methods. Martin Luther King Jr. believed that the only way to gain full equality for his people was to do the same thing.

In 1959, he made a pilgrimage to India, visited Gandhi's tomb, and further studied Gandhi's principles of nonviolence. Since he was a minister, Dr. King added to these principles his belief in Christian love and brotherhood.

Throughout his life, he always preached and spoke of this philosophy as the only means towards the goals that his people had set for themselves:

Montgomery, 1955-56

Hate begets hate; violence begets violence. Toughness begets a greater toughness. . . .

23

We must not return violence under any condition. I know this is difficult advice to follow, especially since we have been the victims of no less than ten bombings. But this is the way of Christ; it is the way of the Cross. We must somehow believe that unearned suffering is redemptive. . . .

We will match your capacity to inflict suffering with our capacity to endure suffering. We will meet your physical force with soul force. We will not hate you, but we cannot in all good conscience obey your unjust laws. Do to us what you will and we will still love. . . . But we will soon wear you down by our capacity to suffer. And in winning our freedom we will so appeal to your heart and conscience that we will win you in the process.

Birmingham, 1963

Nonviolence is a powerful and just weapon. It is a weapon unique in history, which cuts without wounding and ennobles the man who wields it. It is a sword that heals. . . .

St. Paul's Cathedral, London, 1964

All over the world as we struggle for justice and freedom, we must never use second class methods to gain it. . . . We must never substitute our oppression for another kind of oppression. . . .

Convent Avenue Baptist Church, New York, 1968

We need an alternative to riots and to timid supplication. Nonviolence is our most potent weapon. . . .

Memphis march, March 30, 1968

Riots are part of the ugly atmosphere of our society. I cannot guarantee that riots will not take place this summer. I can only guarantee that *our* demonstrations will not be violent. . . .

BIRMINGHAM:
FORTRESS OF SEGREGATION

In 1963, seven years after the Montgomery bus boycott had ended, Birmingham, Alabama, was still one of the most segregated cities in the United States. Negroes could not eat in restaurants, play in the public parks, attend nonsegregated schools, or even receive equal treatment in the city's hospitals. The local government was strongly opposed to granting the Negro his civil rights.

The Negroes of this city united under the leadership of Dr. King and his Southern Christian Leadership Conference (SCLC). In Birmingham, the Negro community decided to use the nonviolent techniques of marches, sit-ins, and boycotts to demonstrate against discrimination.

On April 12, 1963, a group of fifty Negroes led by Dr. King marched from Zion Hill Church towards the center of Birmingham. Dr. King and his followers were deliberately disobeying a court injunction against the march. They intended to submit to arrest. Before white

officials would talk to the leaders, more than two thousand demonstrators were jailed.

Dr. King was among the first to be arrested. He was placed in solitary confinement. Despite this, he did not despair. On scraps of paper he wrote to those who criticized him:

My Dear Fellow Clergymen:
I am in Birmingham because injustice is here. . . . I cannot sit idly by in Atlanta and not be concerned about what happens in Birmingham. Injustice anywhere is a threat to justice everywhere. . . . Anyone who lives inside the United States can never be considered an outsider anywhere within its bounds. . . .

We have waited for more than 340 years for our constitutional and God-given rights. . . . Perhaps it is easy for those who have never felt the stinging darts of segregation to say, "Wait." But when you have seen vicious mobs lynch your mothers and fathers at will and drown your sisters and brothers at whim; when you have seen hate-filled policemen curse, kick, and even kill your brothers and sisters; when you see the vast majority of your twenty million Negro brothers smothering in an airtight cage of poverty in the midst of an affluent society . . . when you are harried by day and haunted by night by the fact that you are a Negro, living constantly at tiptoe stance . . . when you are forever fighting a degenerating sense of "nobodiness"— then you will understand why we find it difficult to wait. . . .

One may well ask: "How can you advocate breaking some laws and obeying others?" The answer lies in the fact that there are two types of laws: just and unjust. I would be the first to advocate obeying just laws. One has not only a legal but a moral responsibility to obey just laws. Conversely, one has a moral responsibility to disobey unjust laws. I would agree with St. Augustine that "an unjust law is no law at all." . . .

One who breaks an unjust law must do so openly, lovingly . . . and with a willingness to accept the penalty. I submit that an individual who breaks a law that conscience tells him is unjust, and who willingly accepts the penalty of imprisonment in order to arouse the conscience of the community over its injustice, is in reality expressing the highest respect for law. . . .

BROTHERHOOD:
I HAVE A DREAM

On August 28, 1963, one hundred years after President Abraham Lincoln had signed the Emancipation Proclamation freeing the slaves, there was a great march on Washington. Two hundred thousand people, white and black, came to the capital of the United States to express their belief in integration and full equality for the Negro. Millions more watched on television.

Different leaders of the civil rights organizations addressed the throng that had gathered in West Potomac Park facing the white marble columns of the Lincoln Memorial. The words "peace" and "freedom," "love" and "understanding," soared through the air beyond the steeple of the Washington Monument.

But it was Martin Luther King Jr. whom these thousands had waited to hear. Often he had spoken of brotherhood and his hopes for the future. Never before had so many seemed so eager to receive his words. Dr. King moved to the rostrum, saying:

I say to you today, even though we face the difficulties of today and tomorrow, I still have a dream. It is a dream deeply rooted in the American Dream. I have a dream that one day this nation will rise up, live out the true meaning of its creed: "We hold these truths to be self-evident, that all men are created equal."

I have a dream that one day on the red hills of Georgia the sons of former slaves and the sons of former slaveowners will be able to sit down together at the table of brotherhood.

I have a dream that one day even the state of Mississippi, a desert state sweltering with the heat of injustice and oppression, will be transformed into an oasis of freedom and justice.

I have a dream that my four little children will one day live in a nation where they will not be judged by the color of their skin but the content of their character.

I have a dream today.

I have a dream that one day the state of Alabama . . . will be transformed into a situation where little black boys and little black girls will be able to join hands with little white boys and white girls and walk together as sisters and brothers.

I have a dream today.

I have a dream that one day every valley shall be exalted, every hill and mountain shall be made low. The rough places will be made plain, and the crooked places will be made straight. . . .

This is the faith with which I return to the South.

With this faith we will be able to hew out of the mountain of despair a stone of hope. . . . With this faith we will be able to work together . . . knowing we will be free one day.

This will be the day when all of God's children will be able to sing with new meaning . . . "let freedom ring." . . . So let freedom ring from the hilltops of New Hampshire. Let freedom ring from the mighty mountains of New York. . . . But not only that. Let freedom ring from Stone Mountain of Georgia. Let freedom ring from every hill and molehill of Mississippi, from every mountain side. . . .

When we allow freedom to ring—when we let it ring from every village and every hamlet, from every state and every city, we will be able to speed up that day when all of God's children, black men and white men, Jews and Gentiles, Protestants and Catholics, will be able to join hands and sing in the words of the old Negro spiritual, "Free at last, Free at last, Thank God Almighty, we are free at last."

THE NOBEL PEACE PRIZE

On December 10, 1964, Dr. Martin Luther King Jr. stood before the King of Norway, the Crown Prince, government and diplomatic leaders, members of his family and associates of the civil rights movement to accept the Nobel Prize for Peace. People throughout the world watched as he accepted the award on television.

Dr. King was the third member of his race to receive this award and the youngest to be so honored.

In a slow, deeply moving voice that resounded in the great marble halls of the University of Oslo, he accepted the award, saying:

I accept the Nobel Prize for Peace at a moment when twenty-two million Negroes of the United States of America are engaged in a creative battle to end the long night of racial injustice. . . .

I am mindful that only yesterday in Birmingham, Alabama, our children, crying out for brother-

hood, were answered with fire hoses, snarling dogs, and even death. . . .

I am mindful that . . . grinding poverty afflicts my people and chains them to the lowest rung of the economic ladder.

Therefore, I must ask why this prize is awarded to a movement which is beleaguered and committed to unrelenting struggle; to a movement which has not won the very peace and brotherhood which is the essence of the Nobel Prize. After contemplation, I conclude that this award which I receive on behalf of that movement is a profound recognition that nonviolence is the answer to the crucial political and moral question of our time. . . .

Sooner or later, all the people of the world will have to discover a way to live together in peace. . . .

If this is to be achieved, man must evolve for all human conflict a method which rejects revenge, aggression and retaliation.

The foundation of such a method is love. . . .

I accept this award today with an abiding faith in America and an audacious faith in the future of mankind. . . .

I refuse to accept the view that mankind is so tragically bound to the starless midnight of racism and war that the bright daybreak of peace and brotherhood can never become a reality. . . .

I have the audacity to believe that **peoples** everywhere can have three meals a day for their bodies, education and culture for their minds, and dignity, equality and freedom for their spirits. I believe that what self-centered men have torn down, men other-centered can build up. . . . I still believe that we shall overcome.

This faith can give us courage to face the uncertainties of the future. It will give our tired feet new strength as we continue our forward stride toward the city of freedom. When our days become . . . darker than a thousand midnights, we will know that we are living in the creative turmoil of a genuine civilization struggling to be born. . . .

I accept this prize on behalf of all men who love peace and brotherhood. I say I come as a trustee, for in the depths of my heart, I am aware that this prize is much more than an honor to me personally. . . .

I think Alfred Nobel would know what I mean when I say that I accept this award in the spirit of a curator of some precious heirloom which he holds in trust for its true owners—all those to whom beauty is truth and truth beauty—and in whose eyes the beauty of genuine brotherhood and peace is more precious than diamonds or silver or gold.

THE RIGHT TO VOTE:
SELMA TO MONTGOMERY

One of the most precious rights of every American citizen is the right to vote. In 1965, Dr. King returned to Alabama to help his people gain this right in full measure. Although there had been amendments to the Constitution since the Negro had been a free man, many still were unable to exercise the basic right to vote.

In order to make this struggle more dramatic, Dr. King organized a march from Selma to Montgomery. There was much violent and brutal opposition by the white authorities to this march. Thousands of people throughout the United States and Europe were so shocked by the tactics of the police that they decided to join Dr. King's march.

On March 25, 1965, at the end of the fifty-four mile march, Dr. King spoke to twenty-five thousand people who had gathered in the state capital to show their support of the civil rights movement. There were people from all walks of life—clergymen, college students,

television and motion picture stars. The words of Martin Luther King Jr. rang out across the state, the nation, and the world. He spoke for his people, saying:

Last Sunday more than eight thousand of us started on a mighty walk from Selma, Alabama. We have walked on meandering highways and rested our bodies on rocky byways. Some of our faces are burned from the outpouring of the sweltering sun. Some have slept in the mud. We have been drenched by the rains. Our bodies are tired and our feet are somewhat sore. . . .

They told us we wouldn't get here. And there are those who said that we would get here only over their dead bodies, but, all the world knows today that we are here and that we are standing before the forces of power in the state of Alabama singing, "We ain't goin' let nobody turn us around."

There never was a moment in American history more honorable and more inspiring than the pilgrimage of clergymen and laymen of every race and faith pouring into Selma to face danger at the side of its embattled Negroes.

On our part we must pay our profound respects to the white Americans who cherish their democratic traditions over the ugly customs and privileges of generations and come forth boldly to join hands with us. . . .

So I stand before you this afternoon with the conviction that segregation is on its death bed in Alabama and the only thing uncertain about it is how costly the segregationist will make the funeral. . . .

Our whole campaign in Alabama has been centered around the right to vote. In focusing the attention of the nation and the world today on the flagrant denial of the right to vote, we are exposing the very origin, the root cause of racial segregation in the Southland.

Today I want to tell the city of Selma—today I want to say to the state of Alabama—today I want to say to the people of America and the nations of the world: we are not about to turn around. We are on the move now. Yes, we are on the move and no wave of racism can stop us. We are on the move now. . . .

Let us march on the ballot boxes until we send to our city councils, state legislatures and the United States Congress, men who will not fear to do justice, love mercy and walk humbly with their God. Let us march on the ballot boxes until all over Alabama God's children will be able to walk the earth in decency and honor. . . .

My people, my people listen. The battle is in our hands. . . .

So as we go away this afternoon, let us go away more than ever before committed to nonviolence. . . . We are still in for a season of suffering. . . .

I must admit to you there are still jail cells waiting for us, dark and difficult moments. We will go on with the faith in nonviolence and its power that transformed dark yesterdays into bright tomorrows. We will be able to change all conditions. . . .

Our aim must never be to defeat or humiliate the white man but to win his friendship and understanding. We must come to see that the end we seek is a society of peace. . . . That will be the day not of the white man, not of the black man. That will be the day of man as man.

I know you are asking today, "How long will it take?. . . ."

How long? Not long because no lie can live forever.

How long? Not long because you will reap what you sow.

How long? Not long because the arm of the universe is long but it bends towards justice.

How long? Not long. . . .

I OPPOSE THE WAR

Dr. King was criticized by both whites and blacks for opposing the war in Vietnam. Some said it was wrong to take time away from the civil rights struggle for other causes. Dr. King answered those who spoke against him:

Chicago, March 1967

America is a great nation, but she seems bent on her destruction. Through rugged and dazzling achievements, America has become the richest and most powerful nation in the world. We have built machines that think and instruments that peer into space. We have built bridges to span the seas and gigantic buildings to kiss the skies. . . . All of this is a staggering picture of our great power. . . .

But honesty impels me to admit that our power has often made us arrogant. We feel that our money can do anything. We feel that we have everything to teach other nations and nothing to learn from them. We often feel that we have some divine mission to police the whole world. We are arrogant in not allowing young nations to go through the same growing pains and revolutions that characterize our history. . . .

We arm Negro soldiers to kill on foreign battlefields, but offer little protection for their relatives in our own South. We are willing to make the Negro 100 per cent of a citizen in warfare, but reduce him to 50 per cent of a citizen on American soil. Of all good things in life, the Negro has approximately one-half those of the whites. Of the bad he has twice that of the whites. . . .

Let me say, that I oppose the war because I love America. I speak out against it not in anger but with anxiety and sorrow in my heart and above all with a passionate desire to see our beloved country stand as a moral example to the world.

I speak out against war because I am disappointed with America. There can be no great disappointment where there is no great love.

I am disappointed with our failure to deal positively and forthrightly with the triple evils of racism, materialism and militarism. . . .

Those who love peace must organize as effectively as the war hawks. As they spread the propaganda of war, we must spread the propaganda of peace. We must combine the fervor of the civil rights movement and the peace movement. We must demonstrate, teach, and preach until the very foundations of our nation are shaken. We must work unceasingly to lift this nation that we love to a higher destiny. . . .

Riverside Church, New York City: April 4, 1967

Somehow this madness must cease. We must stop now. I speak as a child of God. . . . I speak for those whose land is being laid waste, whose homes are being destroyed. I speak for the poor of America who are paying the double price of smashed hopes at home and death and corruption abroad. I speak as a citizen of the world, for the world as it stands aghast at the path we have taken. I speak as an American to the leaders of my own nation. The great initiative in this war is ours. The initiative to stop it must be ours. . . .

POVERTY:
THE FINAL CRUSADE

Dr. King felt deeply that no man should suffer the harsh pain of poverty, especially in the richest country in the world. It was with this belief that he planned a second march on Washington—a "Poor People's March" to dramatize the plight of the poor to Congress and to the other branches of the government. As before, Dr. King spoke of what was in his heart to the people of the nation:

Montgomery, Alabama, March 25, 1965

Let us march on poverty until no American parent has to skip a meal so that his children, too, must march on poverty. Until no starved man walks the streets of the cities and towns in search of jobs that do not exist. . . .

Grenada, Mississippi, March 20, 1968

Even though Quitman County [Marks, Mississippi] is the poorest in the United States, it is still criminal for people to have to live in these conditions. I am very deeply touched. God does not want you to live like you are living. . . .

Memphis, Tennessee, March 31, 1968

It will be a long and difficult struggle, for our program calls for a redistribution of economic power. . . . I feel this movement on behalf of the poor is the most moral thing—it is saying that every man is an heir to a legacy of dignity and worth. . . .

No, the rich man was punished because he passed Lazarus everyday and did not see him and I tell you if this country does not see its poor—if it lets them remain in poverty and misery—it will surely go to Hell. . . .

Just as in 1963, the majority desired action on civil rights for the Negro, so most people now agree that poverty has to be wiped out. . . .

A MARKED MAN

Although Martin Luther King Jr. was the champion of nonviolence, he was forced to live with the constant threat of danger. Dr. King and his family received telephone threats continually. His home was bombed several times.

On April 3, 1968, Dr. King addressed the striking sanitation workers of Memphis. He was greatly disturbed by the violence which had been caused by his marchers. Speaking in the tone of a man who felt marked for death, Dr. King said:

I left Atlanta this morning, and as we got started on the plane—there were six of us—the pilot said over the public address system: "We're sorry for the delay but we have Dr. Martin Luther King on the plane. . . . And to be sure that nothing would be wrong on the plane, we had to check out everything carefully. And we've had the plane protected and guarded all night."

And then I got into Memphis. And some began to say the threats—or talk about the threats that were out. Or what would happen to me from some of our sick white brothers.

Well, I don't know what will happen now. We've got some difficult days ahead. But it really doesn't matter with me now. Because I've been to the mountain top. I won't mind.

Like anybody, I would like to live a long life. . . . But I'm not concerned about that now. I just want to do God's will.

And He's allowed me to go up to the mountain. And I've looked over, and I've seen the promised land. I may not get there with you, but I want you to know tonight that we as a people will get to the promised land.

So I'm happy tonight. I'm not worried about anything. I'm not fearing any man. "Mine eyes have seen the glory of the coming of the Lord. . . ."

CALL ME A DRUM MAJOR

*I*n February of 1968, Martin Luther
King Jr. delivered a sermon to his parishoners at the
Ebenezer Baptist Church. In this sermon he spoke
about his life and what he would like to be remembered
for after his death. Dr. King preached to the congre-
gation, saying:

> If any of you are around when I have to meet
> my day, I don't want a long funeral. . . .
> And if you get somebody to deliver the eulogy
> tell him not to talk too long.
> And every now and then I wonder what I want
> him to say. . . .
> I'd like somebody to mention that day that Mar-
> tin Luther King Jr. tried to give his life serving
> others.
> I'd like somebody to say that day that Martin
> Luther King Jr. tried to love somebody.
> I want you to say that day I tried to be right and

I went you to say that day I tried to be right and

to walk with them. I want you to be able to say that day that I did try to feed the hungry. I want you to be able to say that day that I did try in my life to clothe the naked. I want you to say on that day that I did try in my life to visit those who were in prison. And I want you to say that I tried to love and serve humanity.

Yes, if you want to say that I was a drum major for peace. I was a drum major for righteousness.

And all of the other shallow things will not matter. . . .

HIS DEATH

On April 4, 1968, while he was speaking to a friend from the balcony of the Lorraine Motel in Memphis, Dr. King was shot. The assassin's bullet smashed through his neck and exploded against his lower right jaw. One hour later, Dr. Martin Luther King Jr. died in St. Joseph's Hospital.

Words of shock and messages of sorrow came to his family in Atlanta from all over the world. His widow, Mrs. Coretta King, made the arrangements for his funeral. From the White House, the President declared a National Day of Mourning.

On Tuesday, April 9, 1968, the funeral was held in the Ebenezer Baptist Church. Among the many who were present were the Vice President, three United States Senators, governors, church leaders of all faiths, and thirty-five representatives of foreign countries.

After the service, the coffin of Dr. King was placed on a faded green farm wagon pulled by two mules. Mrs. King chose this means of carrying her husband's body

through the streets of Atlanta to show that, even in death, he was still close to the simple, poor people he tried to help. It carried him past the Capitol, through the downtown section, through Negro districts, to Morehouse College for further ceremonies. Finally, it took him to South View Cemetery, where his body would remain temporarily until a permanent place could be made ready at Morehouse College.

"Free at last, Free at last, Thank God Almighty, I'm free at last," was written on his tomb.

Behind the simple farm wagon marched thousands— the high and the humble, the black and the white. Politicians and show business personalities joined hands with tenant farmers and slum dwellers. Together they marched and sang the songs of freedom. Banks, businesses, stores, and schools across the nation were closed to honor a black man—a man whose ancestors were slaves.

A marble plaque was placed on the balcony of the Lorraine Motel to mark the spot where the gentle champion of nonviolence had met his violent end. It carried the inscription:

"THEY SAID ONE TO ANOTHER, BEHOLD HERE COMETH THE DREAMER. LET US SLAY HIM AND WE SHALL SEE WHAT BECOMES OF HIS DREAMS."

INDEX

King, Martin
Luther

323.4
HAR

We shall live
in peace

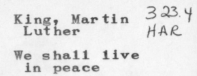

DATE		
FEB 19	MR 30 '01	
MAR 20		
APR 28		
MAY 11		
MAR 27		
FEB 13		
MAR 20 '87		
JAN 28 '87		
NOV 1 9		
DEC 1 6		
MR 06 '01		